I0843464

THANKSGIVING COLORING BOOK
FOR TODDLERS

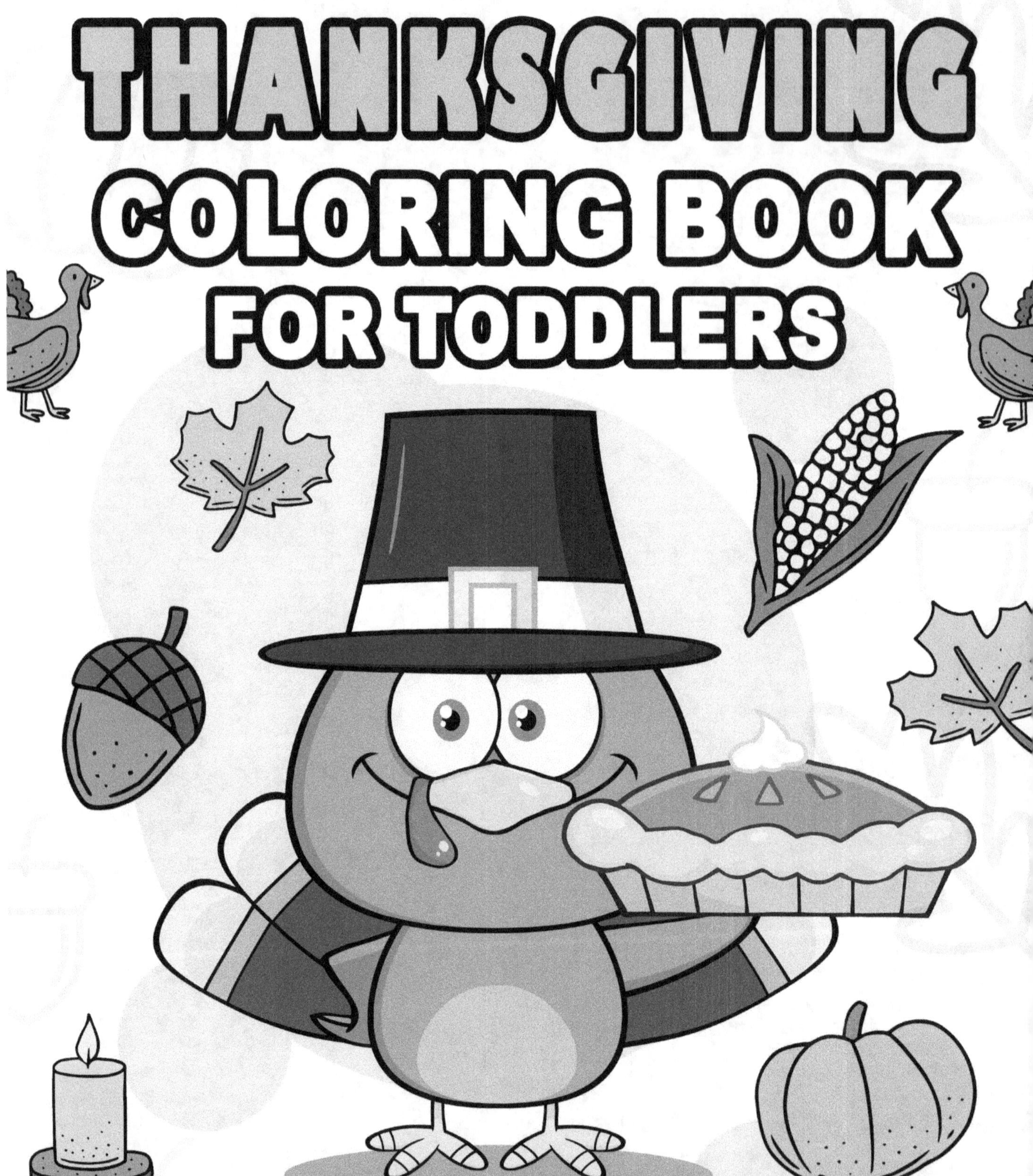

SIMPLE BIG PICTURES HAPPY HOLIDAY COLORING BOOKS FOR KIDS AND PRESCHOOLERS

The Coloring Book Art Design Studio

THANKSGIVING
COLORING BOOK FOR TODDLERS

by The Coloring Book Art Design Studio

THANKSGIVING
COLORING BOOK FOR TODDLERS

THIS BOOK
BELONG TO

____

____

LET'S TEST YOUR COLOR

AUTUMN FESTIVAL
HAPPY
Thanksgiving

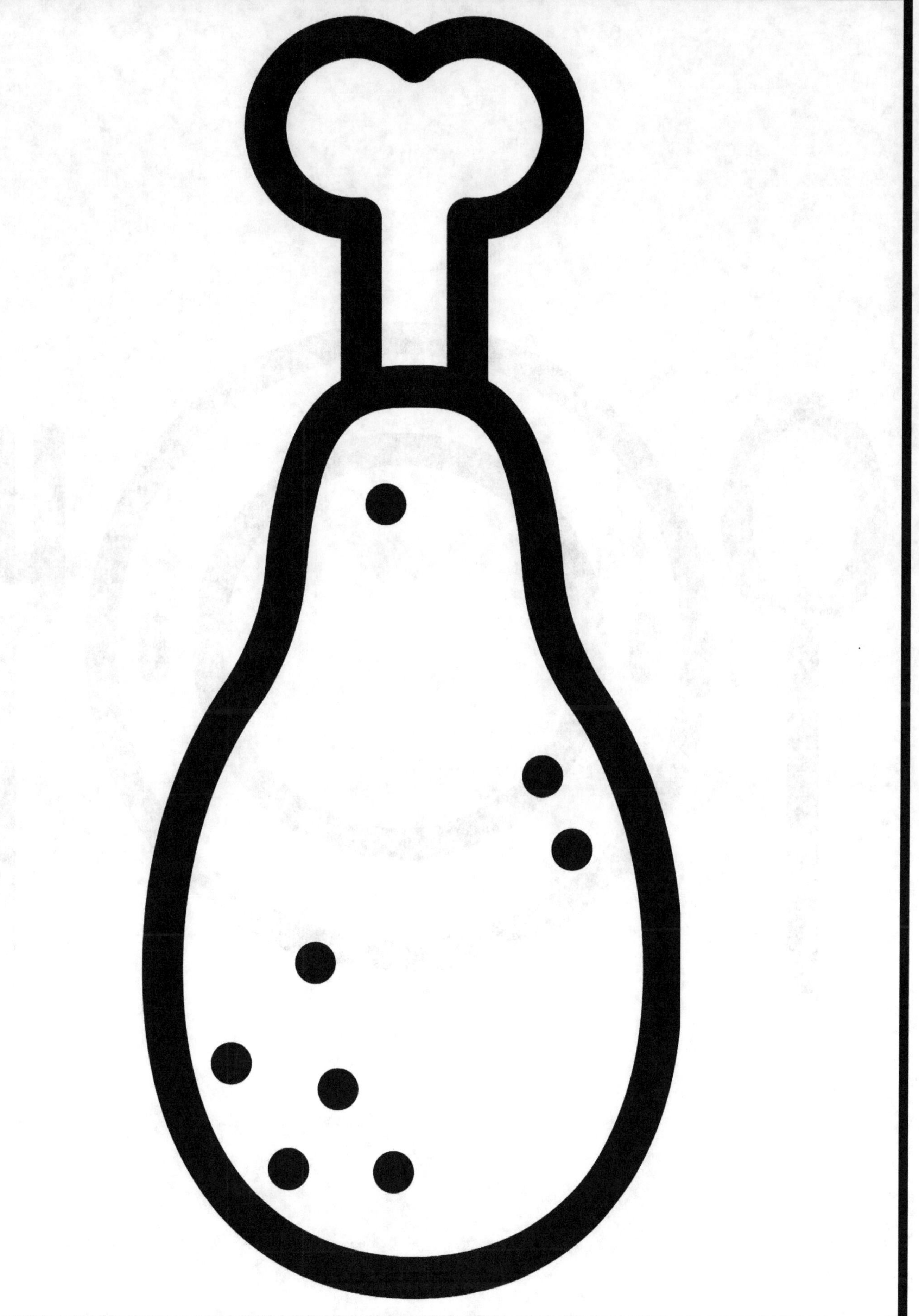

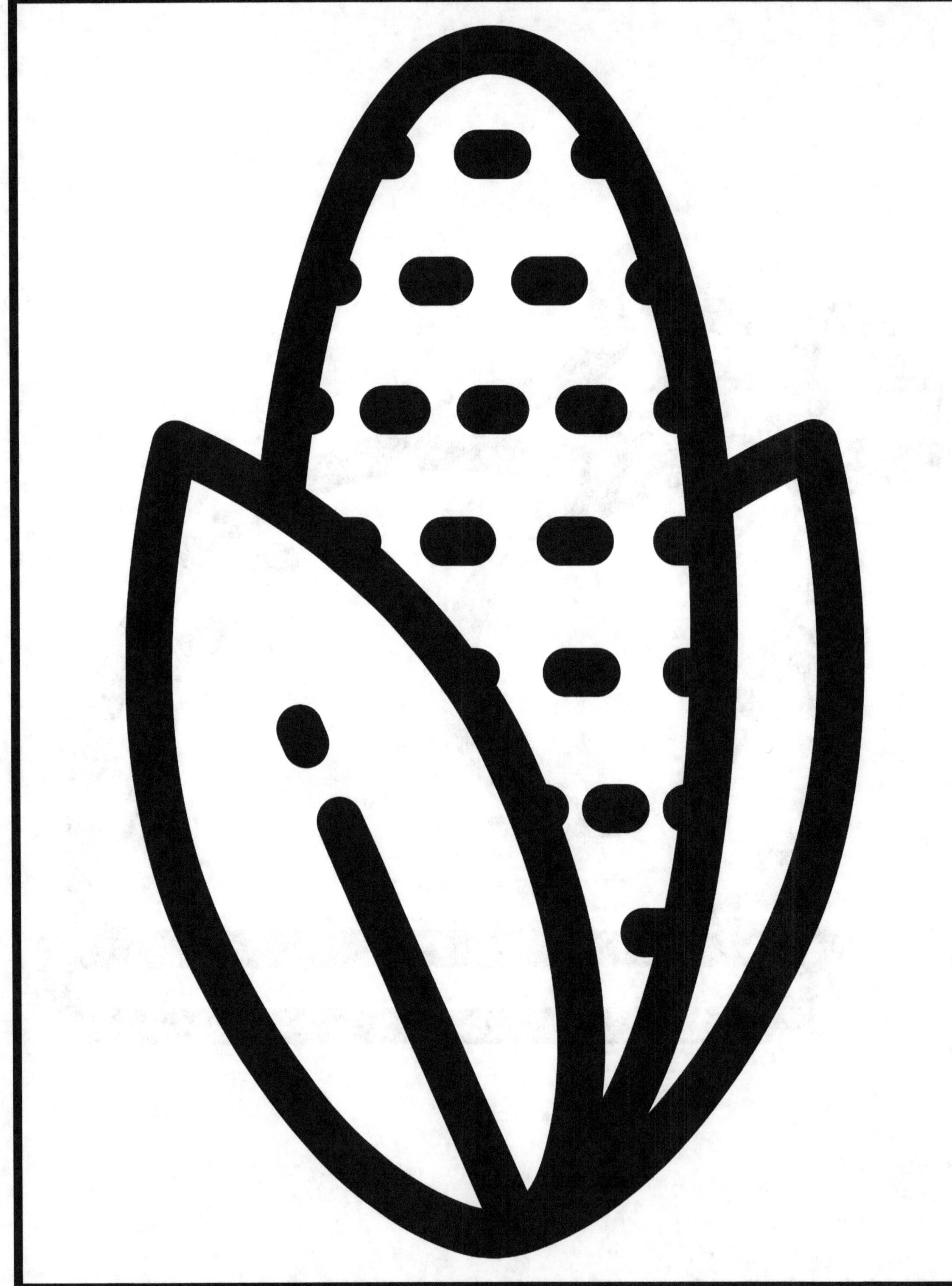

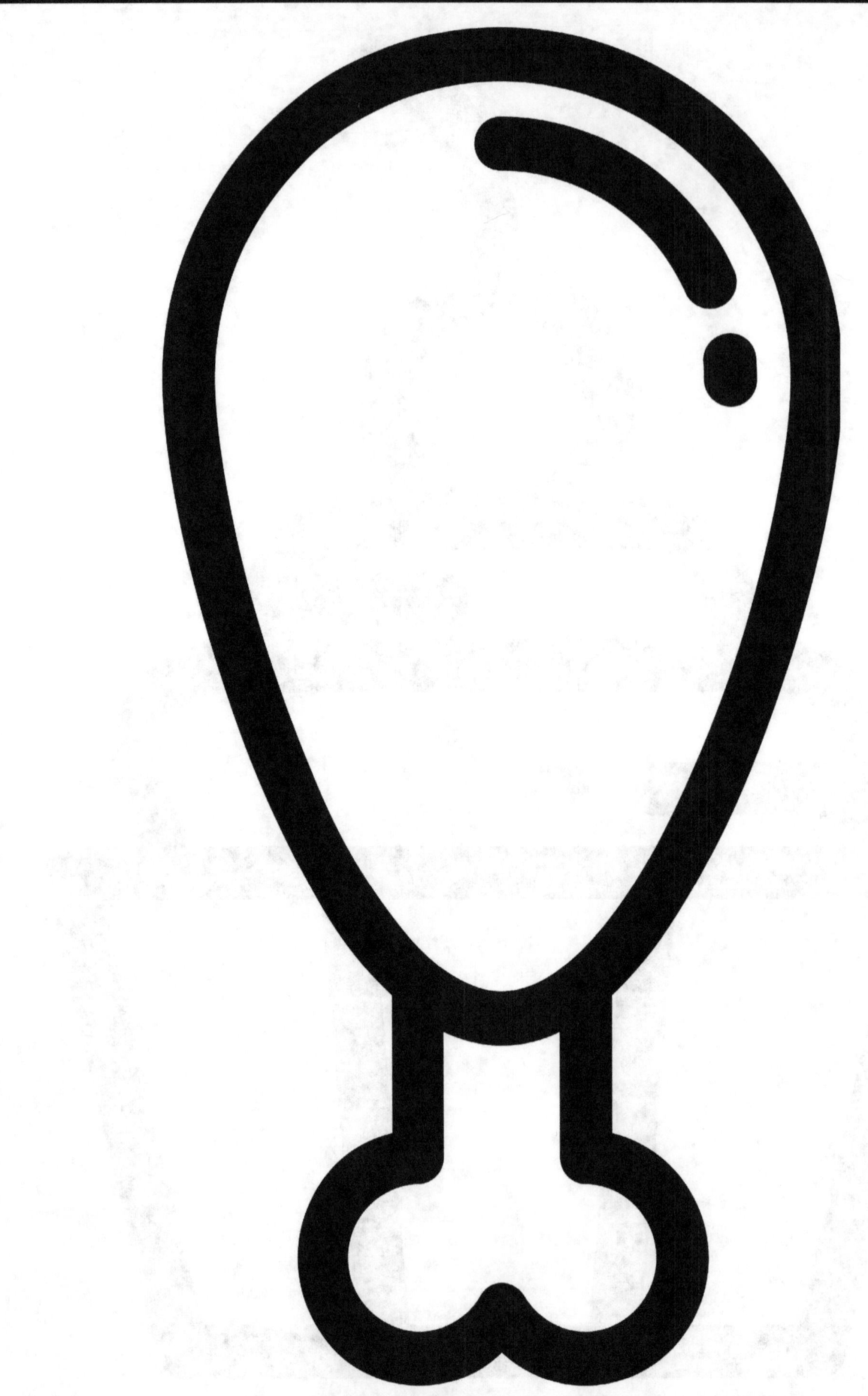

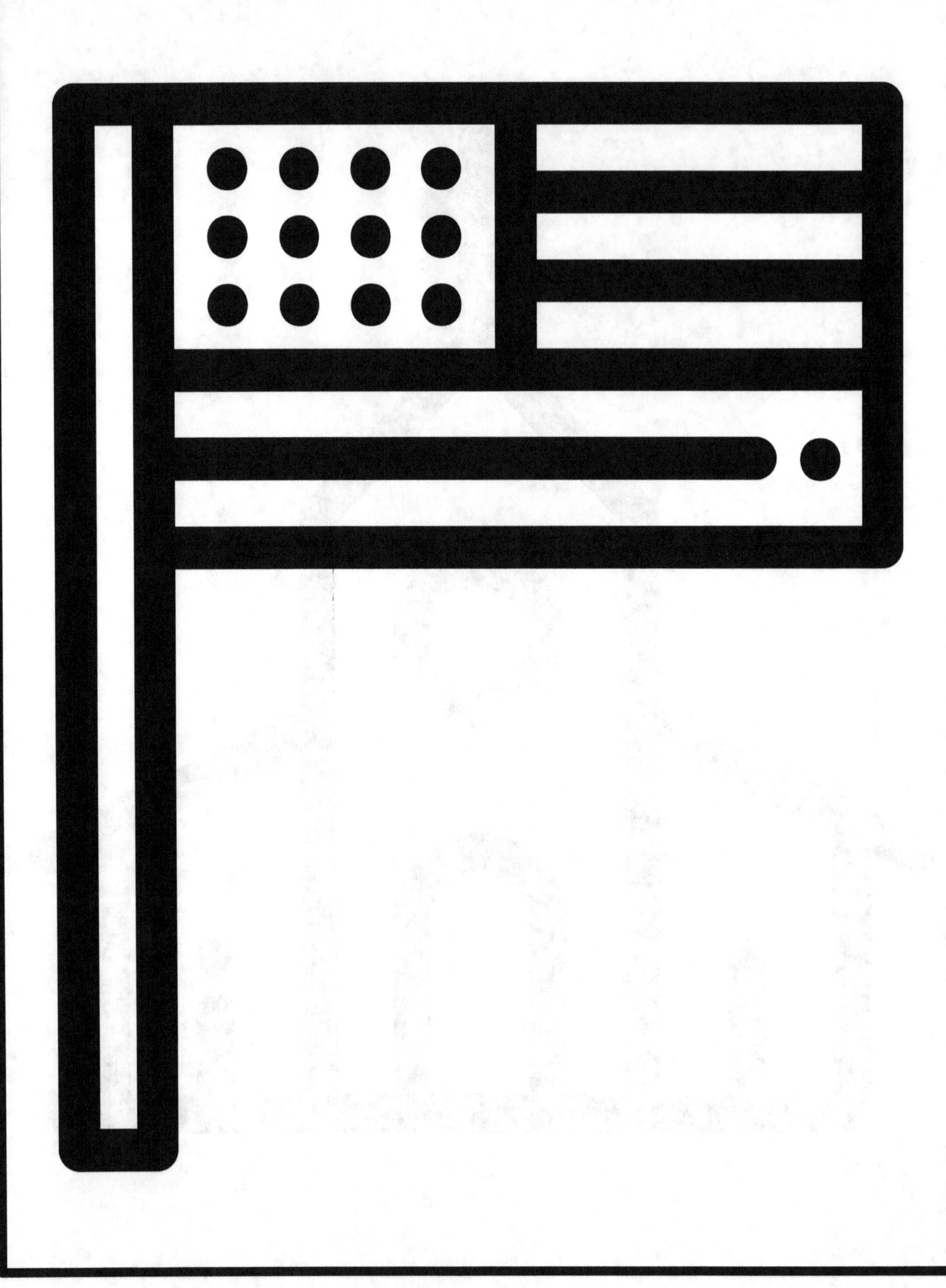

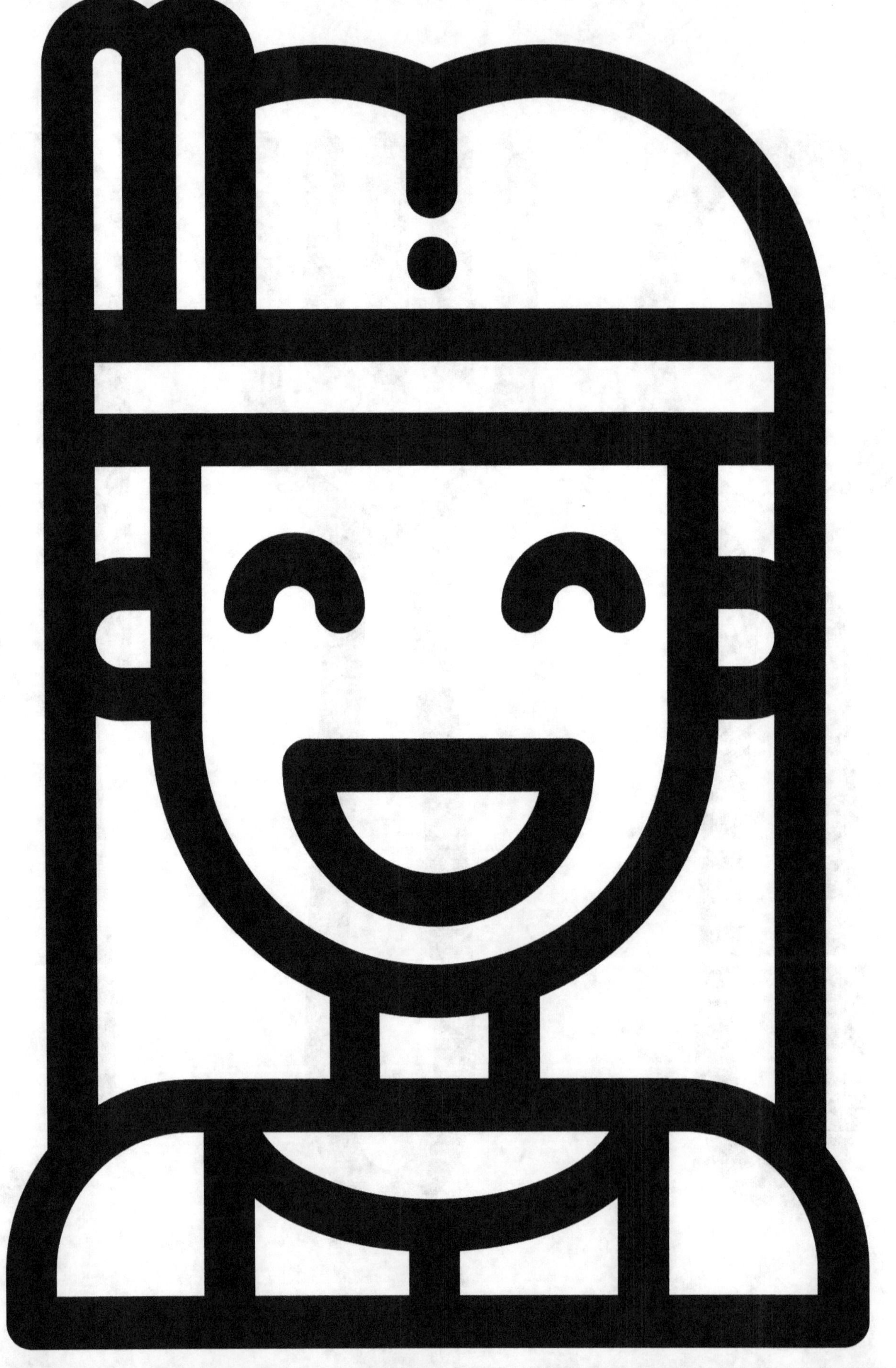

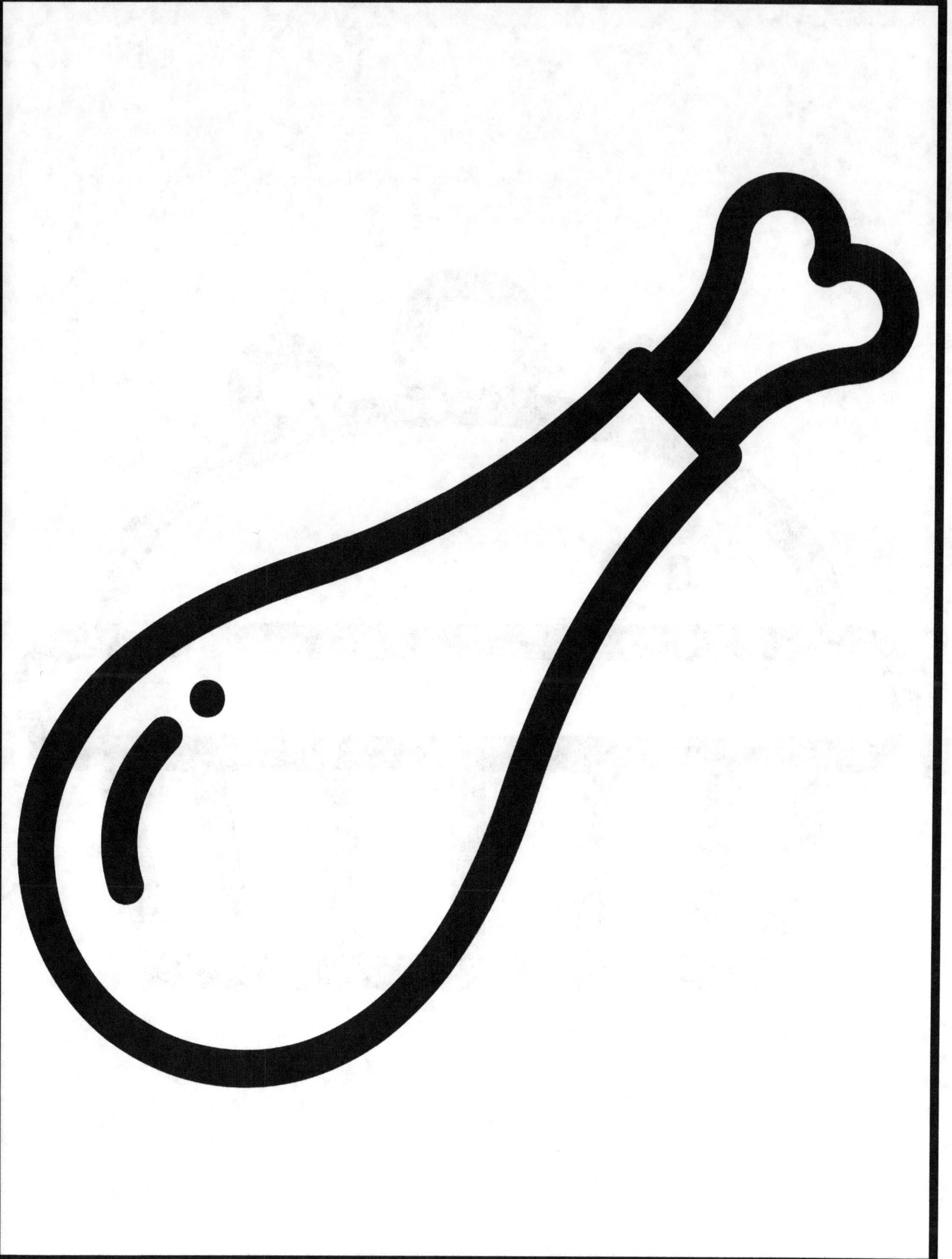

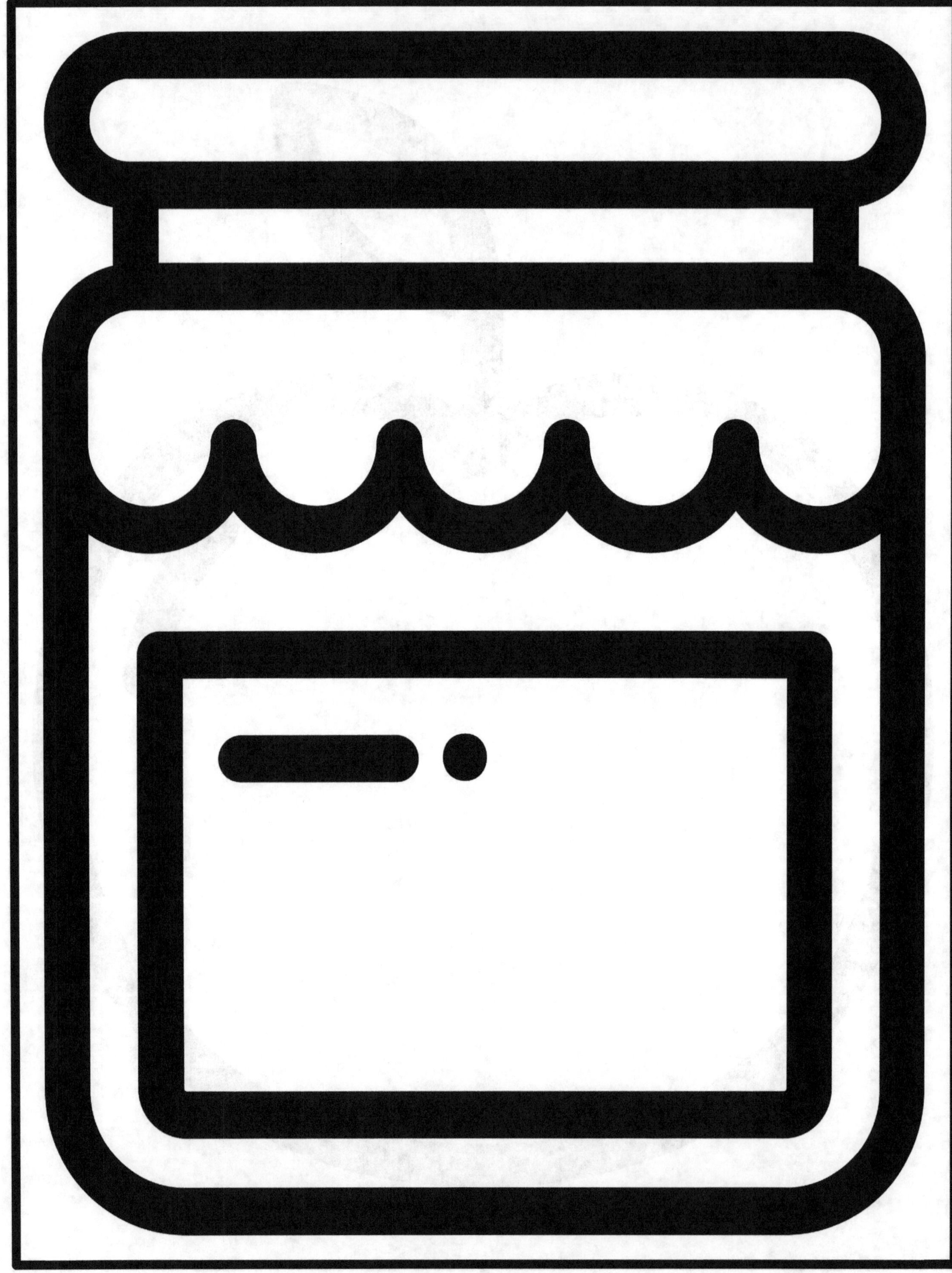

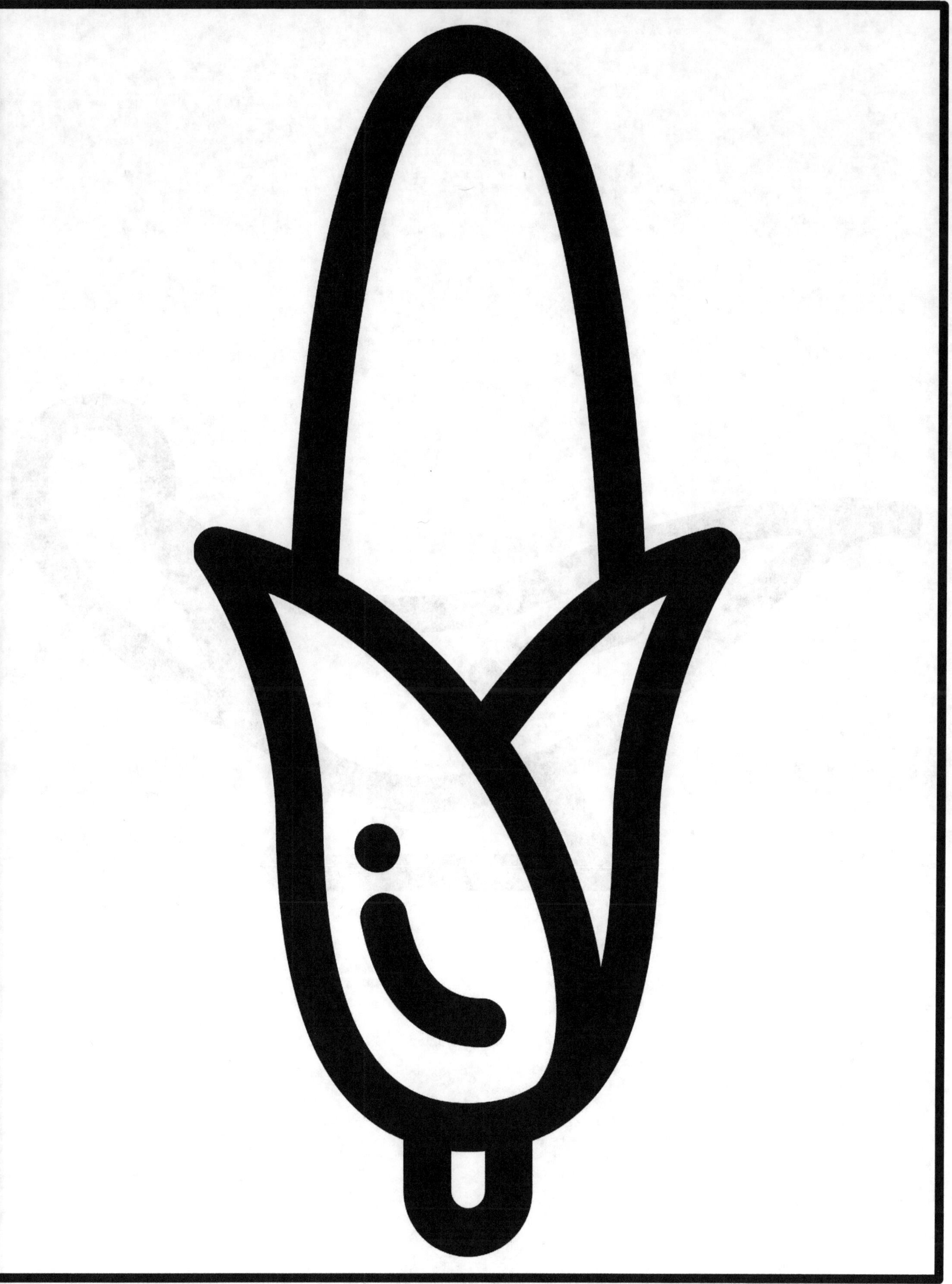

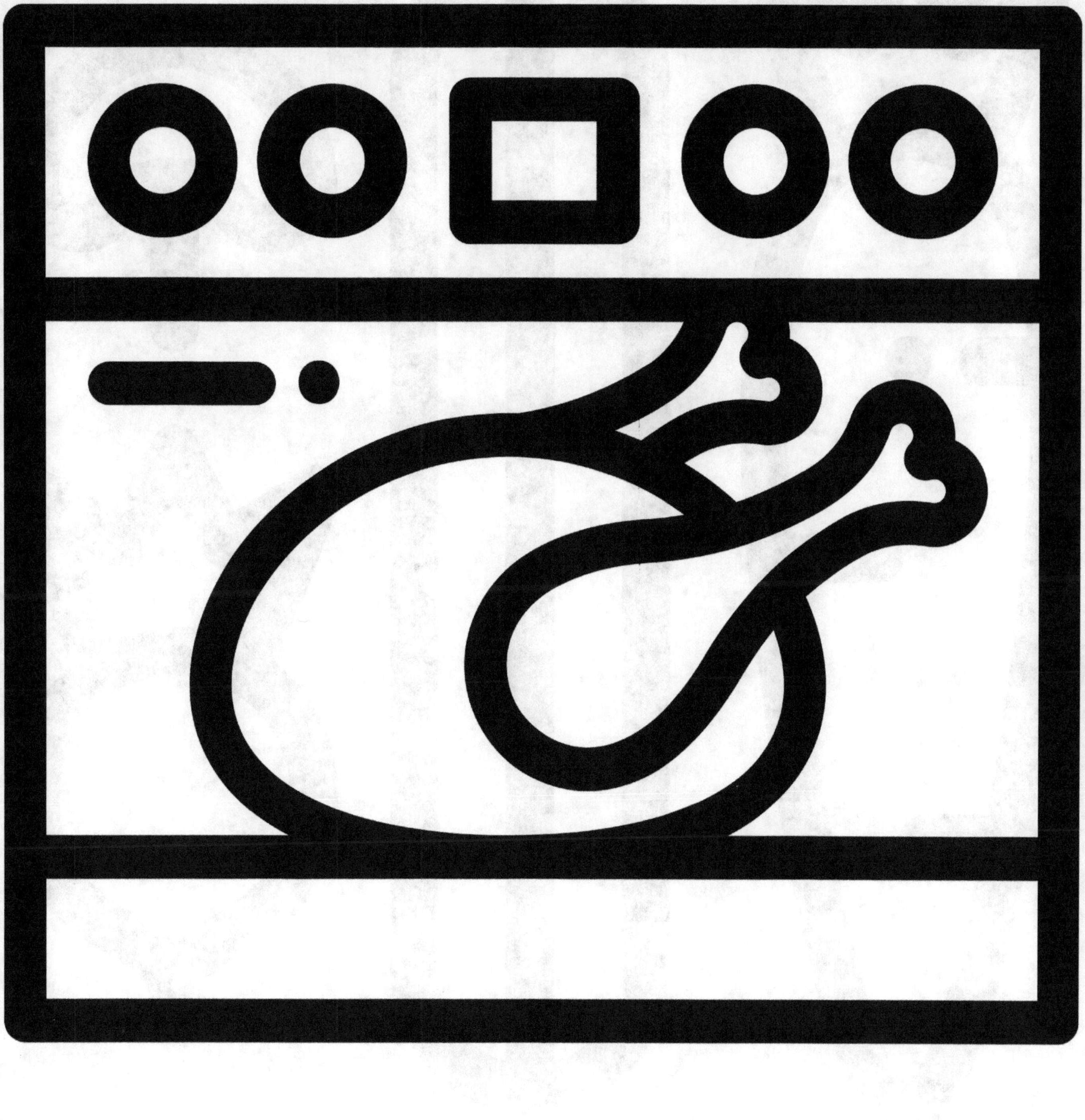

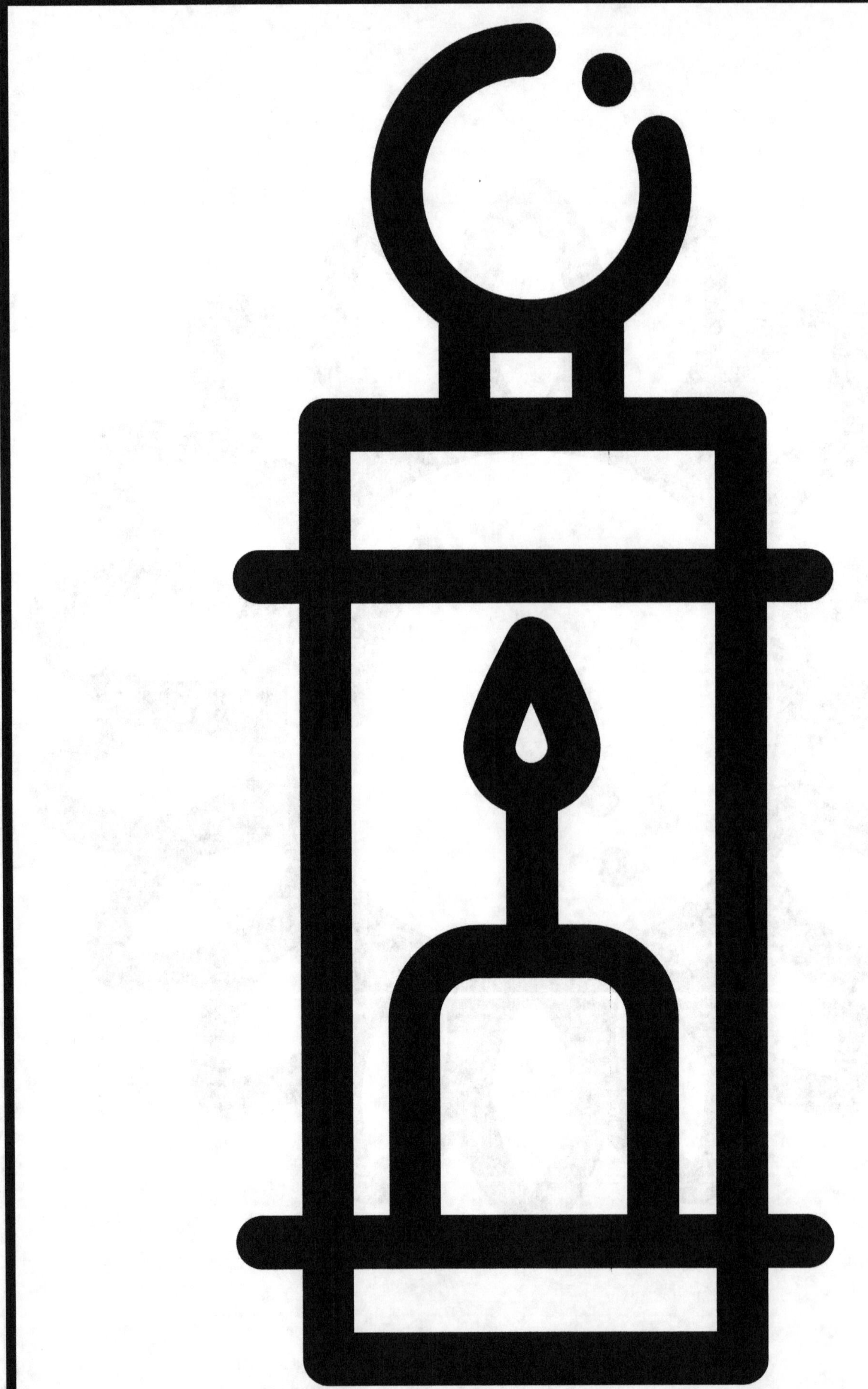

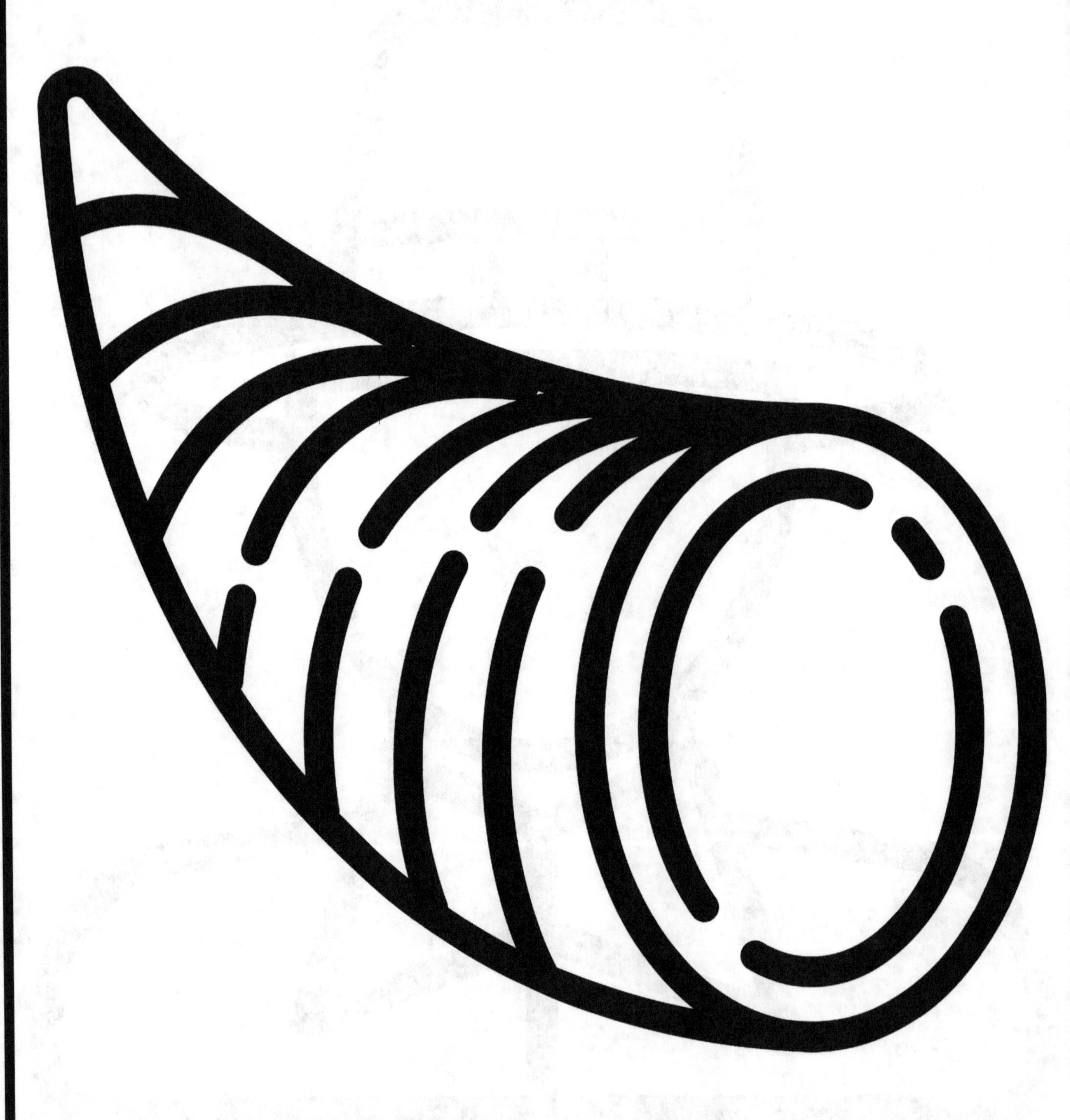

THANKS
GIVING

www.ingramcontent.com/pod-product-compliance
Lightning Source LLC
Chambersburg PA
CBHW081624250726
48657CB00009B/2710